A
Sexual
Tour
of the
Deep
South

A Sexual Tour of the Deep South

poems by
Rosemary
Daniell

HOLT, RINEHART AND WINSTON
New York

Published simultaneously in Canada by Holt, Rinehart
and Winston of Canada, Limited.

Library of Congress Cataloging in Publication Data
Daniell, Rosemary.
A sexual tour of the Deep South.

Poems.
I. Title.
PS3554.A56S4   811'.5'4   74-15473
ISBN 0-03-013721-7 cloth
ISBN 0-03-013726-8 pbk.

*Some of these poems originally appeared in the following publications whose
editors are thanked for permission to reprint:*
Archon: "Tulips"; *Atlantic Monthly*: "Bridal Luncheon"; *DeKalb Literary
Arts Journal*: "Rape of Lilith," "The Victim," "Blood Sherbet," "A Bird Like a
Peacock Downed"; *The Great Speckled Bird*: "The Doll"; *New Orleans Review*:
"Declaration Day," "A Week in February," "The State of Georgia," "Shiksa,"
"Talking of Stars," "Over Chattanooga," "The Bible Salesman," "The Angel
Stud"; *New York Quarterly*: "I Want," "What's Happening"; *Sojourner*: "Girl
Friends"; *Tri-Quarterly*: "Tiger Lilies"; *We Become New: Poems of
Contemporary American Women*, Bantam Books, 1975: "Girl Friends,"
"Before the Fall," "I Want," "To a Family Man in His Family Room."

Grateful acknowledgment is made for use of four lines from "Crazy Jane
Talks with the Bishop" by William Butler Yeats, from *Collected Poems of
William Butler Yeats*, copyright 1924 by The Macmillan Company, renewed
1952 by Bertha Georgie Yeats. Reprinted by permission of The Macmillan
Company.

First Edition
PRINTED IN THE UNITED STATES OF AMERICA

Thanks to the National Endowment for the Arts for their award of a fellowship grant in creative writing for the year 1974–75, during which several of these poems were written.

for my daughters
who are already free women

Contents

Blood Sherbet

A Sexual Tour of the Deep South

Radical Surgery

exorcism: the hysterical womb, the embedded penis

in embryo, the same tissue that forms the vulva makes the scrotum; the tissue that forms the clitoris creates the penis

all women who are not feminists are masochists

What's Happening

She looks like she was split by a hatchet.
Construction worker, observing photo
of nude woman

1

is somebody's wrist
a rubber hose
a blackjack   a stob
a bony snout—

              you

2

are the other
who rushes in—
the onlooker at
an accident—
excited by my
cries, pleased by
my severed limb.
Glad of your own,
and mean enough
to stir a gash
with a stick.

3

O who would want to be probed near
the heart by the horn of a bull?
I am soft and used to my wounds,
a crushed thing, weeping tears or blood—

an inversion, the letter V,
a V-letter, a lower form
with one center, an amoeba,
lacking cartilage, or shape—

I fold around hard things, pulsate,
beg. When I'm lucky, I'm fed.

4

In this forest of limbs,
one springs from a twig, rams
upward. From one end to the
other, my body jams—

5

I make a creed:
daily, I force you
to observe my wound.
I move as a slave,
dumbly, bend over—
my dress slides up,
the one under which
I wear *nothing*—
                  I spread
like a rotten spot,
always give way. And
tonight, as I rise
to your command, glide
through darkness, slide
beneath your covers
smelling of honey,
dripping of salt—
I bring the razor.

6

We are the same
now. I love you.

I Want
(ancient history, or a poem archaic
in the story of my life)

no more   no more   to be
this marsh   this piece of liver
this suction   this rubber cup
this leech to your breast,
always sucking too hard. . . .

No. I want to go to Saks,
be clothed in silk & sleek;
have cheeks by Mary Quant,
hair done by Mad Dog John,
my lashes stuck in place
by lacquered fingertips.
I want to lunch with women
in some place dark, expensive—

walk into sunlight
pass the construction hives;
the yellow-hooded guys
to buzz   to ache   tonight
to jerk off or recall me,
fucking their bovine wives. . . .

I want to come home.
I want some other man
to call me on the phone—
to go out to dinner
with friends who are not yours.

Midnight, I want to strip
my Dior slip, pull down
the new silk hose, the ones
bought only for myself—

I want you to see & need.
I want to say, "No, baby,
not tonight." I want
to turn my perfect back
as you did yesterday.

Liturgy

In the restaurant—
Czech & chic—
the first dish
to strike my gaze:
"Rabbits in Cream."
Rabbits: what
high school boys
in Macon, Georgia,
call vaginas—
I see them hopping,
an innocent fieldful,
unknowing how
they'll soon be
skewered   skinned
pierced with forks
in this room
on 72nd Street. . . .

It's Good Friday
& we've been
to Saint Patrick's
at noon   heard
the priest speak
liturgy exotic—
even in English—
to Bible Belt ears

> *"for us   He allowed*
> *Himself   to be bruised*
> *crushed   the nails*
> *to enter His flesh . . ."*

& watched a woman
in plastic rain scarf—

in a silk Givenchy—
in a mantilla of
lace, cheap & stiff—
genuflect to One
who gave Himself

>*to penetration*
>*to mutilation*

as she does each time—
surrounded by the
forests of long
stainless needles
kept in the offices
of rich GYN's—
she's opened like
a purse   knitted
unknitted   vacuumed
& scraped   hooked
like a fish   &
told   "The cervix
has no nerve ends . . ."

each time   forceps
clamp shut   on flesh
as certain   as the
teeth of a trap—
each time she lies—
stunned & skinned
to hear   "This needle
in the perineum
won't hurt   dear . . ."

>*"for us   She allows*
>*Herself   to be bruised*
>*crushed   the nails*
>*to enter Her flesh . . ."*

each time   methi-
olate   is poured
into Her wounds
each time   vinegar
was poured into

> the rabbit   the woman
> her daughter   &
> her daughter's daughter

& standing behind
the pews   I knew
what every woman
there knew   & what
the Pope never has
nor Freud   nor Henry
Miller   nor Nixon
nor William Buckley
nor Norman Mailer—
though maybe Mick
Jagger in lipstick—
that it's not the up-
raised arms   beard
biceps: the power
to push us   into
stirrups   over bath-
tubs   under thumbs
we worship   but what
lies beneath   Her
stained-glass skirts:
cunt   ovaries   womb:
the swollen secret
lips   the soft pink
tits   of Jesus   our
hermaphrodite   our
Sister on the Cross.

Lying There

The deer love to be hunted.
   James Dickey

I set the alarm,
take off my workshirt,
pull up the sheet: *a test tube, a glass*
you turn off the light,
your arm holds my neck,
my hair wets your T-
shirt, you say something
rough; "I smell shampoo. . . ."   *the quiver around*
Stillness. Till you   *the asshole of*
tug away quilts, lift   *the hiding doe*
to hump the fat of
my thigh. Pull up
my legs, push my knees
toward my skull. Now
your blunt flesh probes
the slippery wall,   *a piece of liver*
your fingers part   *a rotten plum*
my lips, your body   *a hog's vulva*
like a fist slips,   *a Georgia swamp*
plunges. Your wrists   *a cave, a cloaca*
force my thighs till   *an O beneath feathers*
the muscles bloom:
through the flame of
stretched red, I feel
your jabs, your final   the shotgun jerks
grunts, your nose   toward the cotton tail
burrows my collarbone: of the frozen female
stranded, unseeing,
crying, I stare   *her paralyzed thighs*
at black leaves through   *the shattered vessel*
the half-closed pane.

Housekeeping

Acid diapers in an open pail—
clogged toilets, sour towels—
the cats shit behind the couch:
my flowers on the table—
my Hothouse Pink slipcovers—
all my House Beautiful tricks—
can't mask the stink, the stink.

> *come in come in   I want you*
> *I will suck you up   I will*
> *eat you: I am made for hard*
> *habitation   rough occupants*

My mother had nests of live rats
in her desk drawers, never
wiped her cunt when she pissed
even before going to Garden
Club. I carry on as she did,
encouraging mildew & dust—
blotting my lipstick on bills—

> *for blows & brute partings*
> *indelicate unsealings—*
> *my entry is a trapdoor*
> *a dark & slanting passage—*

setting glasses on magazines
on the arms of fine oak chairs.
Years ago, Daddy crept out
leaving his fingerprints—
gummy, sweaty. Now every man
who comes here sees them &
thinks how bad my housekeeping

who has the courage to break in
fill me with shoulders & biceps
needle me with slick tattoos
guns   snakes   switchblades?

how messy I am, how unkempt,
how like a sieve, as at noon
my peignoir open & loose—
my nail polish full of holes—
I open the door & he's stuck!
—a fly on flypaper—held
by my Revlon, my stench—

my dream: to have my walls
smashed by blunt knuckles   my
drapes torn   my doorways bruised:
I am happiest when used—

now leaning close for my whisper:
"The meat for supper—rotten.
The milk for breakfast—clotted.
But come in, come in, I want you.
Shove me against the fridge—
for keeping your house, I will
suck you up, I will let you—"

when told "do this"   "do that"
"you are this"   "you are that"
my zero is distraction: it
needs to be filled by your fist.

On Bourbon Street

"She's got tits as hard
as your fist!   Yes sir!
She's tough enough to fuck!"
Mother   he's speaking of
me   your Sonshine   Precious
Boy   now a party of parts—
fake hair & silicone   an
Ideal Doll. Here it's always
Christmas   glitter & tinsel—
I'm gift-wrapped forever.

Wearing a bed jacket with
feathers   I've been probed in
Baton Rouge   purged in New York,
shared a room with a matron
from Westchester   watched her
stitched lids twitch   as I
begged the nurse for a pad—
instead of the sweet snail
you played with   I now have
a gash: Mother   I'm mailing
you my old sex in a box

& I know you'll be thrilled
to hear what I've learned: to
pose in sequins & boa   to
smear on a new kind of mouth—
Ma!   I've got the Revlon
Reds   the Maybelline Blues—
I'm painted-on perfection
a mannequin from Frederick's
the Queen of Bourbon Street.

As bright as a Hiroshima
postcard   Saint Teresa in
a G-string   I dance on high
in this bar   & except for
the bruises of needles   when
my little fanny swishes   I'm
as cute as can be   Mi O Mi!

I'm DYMANITE! I'm Spanish Fly!
I magnetize! *Mother Mother*,
I've got it down by heart now:
the shove to my knees   the dirt
in my face   the nail through
my sex   I'm your daughter
at last   I'm a woman!

Note to Evelyn Mulwray*

*for Dawson Gaillard, speaking of the
feminism of Scarlett O'Hara*

Evelyn   you're everything—
red-lipped   thin-hipped   red-
nailed   veiled   as you order
your vodka tonic   "with lime
instead of lemon":   kept by
a man of means   yet unafraid

to bring beneath your Porthault
sheets   cocks who take your fancy—
such as this overdressed ex-
rookie   whose nose   a slash
of catgut stitches   makes you
itch   sends prickles between
your silk-clad thighs. Evelyn

you're sure to win him: you're
the woman we take lessons from—
on how to wear our *Joy* perfume
on shopping at Lord & Taylor's
on orders to the houseboy. Evelyn

you're all the back issues of
Vogue   a catalog of info
on how to fuck our fathers
on how to o.d. on barbs
stick heads into ovens   lie
on a street in Chinatown—
one eye shot out   a bloody

* Feminine lead, played by Faye Dunaway, in *Chinatown*, a film by Roman
Polanski.

mess on a powdered cheek—
as the daughter we would save
is led away by Daddy—

to learn how to be   red-lipped
thin-hipped   red-nailed   veiled
kept by a man of means.

To Jacquie & the Waitress in Us All

for my sister, Anne

"In 1970 [Jacquie Davison] organized a
national movement against [E.R.A.] and
called it Happiness of Womanhood
(H.O.W.). . . . She is also a writer of sorts,
having published her autobiography . . . *I
Am a Housewife.*
  "In her floor-length baby blue knit
dress with matching beret, with her pale
blonde hair and heavy black eyelashes, she
looked like neither a housewife
nor a lobbyist. . . ."
        Atlanta Journal-Constitution,
        March 17, 1974

"Looking not like a house-
wife"   but a hooker: Jacquie
you haven't beat it yet—
men still call all waitresses
whores   and you know it—
recalling your nights in that
steakhouse in Arizona   cunt
stuffed closed with scripture
from a hundred copies of
True Confessions   the same
issues   in Georgia   I hid
beneath my teenage mattress: *"My first love is a high*
that all of us born with   *school cheerleader,*
the sign between our legs   *Raymond. . . .*
are forever indentured—   *I let him kiss me . . . like I*
deserve our blows   such as   *read in* True Story
your girlhood rape   son out   *magazine."*
of wedlock   Mexican bride-
groom   the one who went berserk,
beat you. . . . Excuse me   sister

I'm confusing your story with
the child I bore at eighteen
my young husband named Ramos
the bruises on my forehead. . . .
Yet Jacquie: pouring coffee
setting down steaks   taking
orders   propositions   must
have been much like   pouring
Coke   rushing out pizza
to students older than me . . .
& stopping at Kiddie Ranch
dragging home to blondine
your hair   repaint your nails—
was that like my two buses
toward my mother's tears   my
son's hot wet diapers   my
dreams from *Glamour* magazine?
Jacquie   you too must have
felt He would never come—
as clear as a saint   wearing
for years   His invisible
foreskin   a ring to keep you. . . .
Till wearing sexy shades   eyes
raping your mascaraed ones
He walked in   asking only
a little regular pussy—
coffee cup filled forever—
& a professional man!
Jacquie   did you too fall
to your knees   ready to suck
off God for the sake of His
name? "Good husband material,"
my mother whispered of my
second   the architect   &
Senora   you knew what side
your bread was buttered on!

"A tall handsome man is
coming into the restaurant . . .
always wearing dark glasses.
I refill his coffee cup. . . ."
"Jacquie was . . . working at
a steakhouse to support
her children when she met
her knight in shining armor."

Each servant needs a master
a woman, her man! But Jacquie:
here our shared story forks:
what happened next to make you
perfect liturgy   service   to
"become as a little child"
rubbing the feet each night
of the man who makes you feel
"like a queen by his side"?   *"Obey him as the*
To make me tear the husband   *little girl . . .*
from my neck like a cross   *when he tells you*
turned green   rebel of words   *something*
novitiate who didn't pan   *it's for your*
out? Yet Jacquie   sister   *own good. . . ."*
love   if today you shed
beehive hair   uplift bra—
if I stepped out of jeans &
sweater   would we recognize
on breasts   belly   thighs
the half-healed wounds   still-fresh
blood: signs of our own whips
of the waitress in us all?

Radical Surgery

Stop fucking and start bleeding.
  Graffiti, women's rest room, Berkeley
  Student Union Building, Berkeley, California

I'm caught in the palm
of an old woman   *as I struggle*
rocking & dipping   *to tear myself*
on her front porch   *off this tree*
on the dirt road—
Mother Superior to the *my surgeon comes*
Convent of the South . . . *a bearded woman*
        whiskers like wire
a soft fleshy trophy   *cud of tobacco*
upright on a stand,
a rod up my spine—
as inside the house
on the table-top
radio, Tammy Wynnette
sings, as Mother grips *wrists as thick*
        as my biceps

me between her knees
like a bottle of
Dr. Pepper, or
a slick ear of corn,
as with ragged nails *a ripper shredder*
she rips down my jeans *with power to force*
pries wide my cunt   *to probe to sever*
        with unwashed fingers
tears out my womb— *white-hot coat wires*
a wet faceless head—
holds it high bleeding
to the toothless man
who sits in the swing

tunelessly humming—
spitting brown juice—

"I al'as loved dolls,"
she cackles, and with
the worn spoon laid by   *the broken necks*
for scraping the corn,   *of drink bottles*
scoops off my breasts
and one at a time, with
rotting teeth, eats.

a long time after
a paper cutout
of my body tries
to lift itself. &
freed of stagnant
sponges   marshes
swamps of blood &
milk: flies   flies

To a Family Man in
His Family Room

Twice during dinner—
the Newburgh, lace napkins—
you left to carpool
at female request.
By the fake fireplace,
your wife clears up in
black velvet pants suit,
jabot of white lace.
Your daughters race
amid the practice
piano, homework
books, parakeet cage,
blasé at meeting
me the live poet
who sits beside you
in jeans & musk—
to lust after, or
confide your reasons:
"I've lived here for
years, engineer at
Redstone Arsenal . . .
great place to raise kids . . ."
Next, your recurring
dream: "I'm in a
house, a known room,
move through a dark
tunnel to another,
full of shapes and
juicy colors, and
wonder why I've
never been there. . . ."

Mister, if you think
I'm about to give
you a guided tour
of rooms I had to
blast my way into—
it's time for my
ride to the airport—
pick up your car keys
along with your balls.
Before I begin
to tell how I had
a house like this
once, a black velvet
pants suit, a son,
and a man as sweet
mild and misled.
And my rage turned
his hair gray, drove
my son insane,
and broke every plate-
glass window in the place.

The Intrauterine Device

Ask the woman who has one.
  My husband, Jon

A good thing we don't share their fear of
sharp instruments near the genitals.
  A housewife

Triangular gold or silver pieces of rocks
are inserted under [the prepuce] to grow
into the skin. . . . The extent of this
painful and dangerous operation, no doubt,
is due to female rule. . . .
  Helen Diner, Mothers and Amazons

Men like to think women come
on the backs of galloping horses—
are mad enough for an animal
prick to be crushed by one—
I pull myself onto your table
prop my soles into stirrups—
you wheel up your stool   adjust
your miner's lamp   stare into
a face unlipsticked   drooling—
smooth on powdered gloves   shove
in the fat tongs   spread them:
doctor   do my thick lips repulse
you who speaks of discharges like
cottage cheese or cloudy water
who cures a thing you've never had
who   face to face with my cunt
neither licks nor kisses
                    only
probes with a stainless needle
(one of sizes through sixteen)
the pencil-dot hole of my womb:

"The flesh here is one-half inch
thick & must be pushed through."
Now   from cellophane   you tear
a fishhook?   an olive pitter?
I try to dream easy fucks—
but recall a boy of ten
ripping a barb from the mouth
of a fish: "They have no nervous
systems," you explain. "Indeed
IUD's were used hundreds of
years ago in Egypt   small gold
wires   or pebbles forced into
the uteri of camels . . ."
                                    doctor
you think it doesn't hurt   you
for whom I dress up: perfume
clean cunt   wedgie shoes   painted
toenails   you   the stranger
willing   for twenty-five bucks
to brave my box with something
rotten in it (a tomato always
in need of chemicals   soap
refrigeration)
                    and as you turn
for leeches?   dildo?   clyster?
some other instrument to root
out evil   I flash a time
when I loved my genitals   when
Amazons roamed the earth   when
I might have gagged you with a fore-
arm   forced you into stirrups
ripped open your trousers
rammed pebbles up your penis:
"A birth control measure, dear . . ."
Instead   I jerk on jeans   shirt—
doctor   is it too late to save

myself from what you're spreading—
a disease worse than vaginitis
cystitis   even pregnancy:
your flaccid-fleshed   pink-plastic-
pricked   money-gorging   cunt-hate?

Cystitis

Blood, you've nailed my clit—
now sting down the small channel
where, in healthier days,
piss flows, clear & pale.
Passing water, I flash easy
streams instead of your crimson
rush, these tears down my cheeks!

Blood, when I swallowed him,
I swallowed diamonds that sank
& sank, cutting my bladder
to this pocketbook full of
you & pus, a small hot purse
embroidered with stones, passed
on by old wives, Mother, the Word.

Blood, you blazon my death:
". . . cancer . . . her belly packed in ice . . ."
White-hot catheters arrive
on trays, carried by an army
of nurses commanded by doctors
wearing badges inscribed,
"Qualified Judge: GOD'S AGENT."

Blood, I'm as caught on your cross
as any farm girl who wakes
in sulfur & haste, begging
mercy for the hand up her skirt
during church, for *later*
in an old Buick: the smell
of rubber, THE SIN, THE SIN.

Blood, I confess, but too late:
in spite of my hot bath, my meal

of tablets, white & chalky,
my fault comes out in *the* spot—
in "a touch of the gravel"—
in "the honeymoon disease"—
in my lover's face, forgotten—

yes, Blood, I'm lightning struck!
in this motel room with Bible—
by the voice of Barbara Walters—
in this stall of blue & tile—
as I squat in your urgent flame,
hellfire of one-night stands,
of women who want too much.

The Operation

Sparse-haired, crumbling
teeth, your old mom
droops from the heat,
the pull on her teats
of a hundred infants.
A worn-out cat,
humped half to death,
she breathes decay
                 so Ruth
            we did it—
you wandered the house,
licked your neat nylon
stitches, your belly
shaved to velvet—

an early spinster
                a young old maid

as I recalled
an operation
in a glass-walled
room at a fair:
a doped dog, carried
in on a tray,
her womb removed,
the strange V shape
held up for the crowd,
knotted with pods
that were puppies . . .

and dreamed of
tiny paws & nails
pink underbellies
scraped-out bodies

the scooping of
ovaries   of
still-closed eyes
yet why
            if that's right
do you now
                  tomgirl
in boots
            chase
the Toms   rush
the tiger lilies
rub against us
singing   singing

as though you're not
dreaming of fuckings,
the taste of placenta,
as though you're not
laughing at my wires
to diaphragm, diapers—
as though you're not
questioning twenty
years of my life?

The Annunciation

Last night, love, you put the cat
beneath your shirt: at work,
I flashed you home cooking, brooding—
how satisfying! Now by simply
blowing, I've made you big—
and, looking up, see your belly—
once flat, black-curled—rise beneath
white cloths: a marshmallow hump,
lump of silly flesh. As those
karate-trained pistons—your
thighs—jerk in leather nets,
your ass wriggles, stirrup-spread
to mirrors, the eyes of student
nurses. Dear, in the bookstore
we stared at pictures of girls
cramped over their red holes—
where will our chick pop from?
Your mouth? Navel? The dark
at the end of . . . your prick
thickens, a homemade sausage
or derma, a cock turned Saran
Wrap as the child shoves downward.
"An episiotomy of the urethra!"
The doctor—a woman, tall,
in white—slashes backward:
of you, nothing stays
but skin, thin, flapping.
O my sweet hermaphrodite!
How your suffering moves me!
Your naked nurse, I lean close
to lick your wounds, to love you.

Note to a Third Husband

    1
baby

    2
though nine years younger
your red beard makes you
the father I never had

    3
and I love
your dirty socks
the freckle by
your left eye
the mole between
your buttocks
                even
your farts.

Before the Fall

When he whirled, the motion was
incredibly swift.
She cried out, just once. . . .
    Frank Yerby, The Saracen Blade

My innocent   my animal
even on your knees
you're my boyfriend
I'm eleven, a girl
with a secret diary
with the small gold key
the fountain pen my
aunt sent from Japan
to hang from its loop
of narrow velvet . . .
with the dark book
on sex, stolen from
Mother & Daddy—
full of pictures
positions   with the
toothbrush holder for
secret masturbation . . .

yes the workshirt you
push from my breasts
is the starter bra
with the blue satin bow
(just a little padded)
is the blue bridal gown
is the shoes dyed to match
is the skirts of six brides-
maids, tutus of blue net
is the ruffle at the base
of each tinted bouquet

is napkins for the shower
is the hope chest towel
embroidered with initials
is the bassinet cover—
blue organdy and ribbons
is the curtain afloat by
my white white appliances
is the calico binding on
my Betty Crocker cookbook
is the potholder that lifts
my cake from the oven, one
of "fifty best recipes" . . .

your hands on my ankles
as bold as my hands
holding yours at twelve
as breathless   rosy
more hopeful than gamblers—
we watch the spin of
a bottle. O your tongue—
as amazing   glorious
strange yes   as our kiss
in the closet, the smell
of camphor & coats . . .
the curls around your ass-
hole as electrifying
as the brass beard of
the pirate, cruel with
lust, in the novels
I devour at fourteen . . .

the dark fur of your
thighs, sign of your
Jewish past—exotic
to mine of Baptist
Sundays   fried chicken

lunches: your mark as
the one I dream as
I flash a world aflame—
how we will spend that
last moment, our bodies
melting together . . .
as the name I carve
on my desk   on my arm
with my pocketknife—
in sequins   with glue
on my thigh   in my diary
year after year after . . .

STRANGER   OTHER   as
your ass in my face
your prick in my mouth
your mouth on my cunt,
you cry out, just once.

A Week in February

1

My host lies naked
in a field by a fence:
to make wine for my
breakfast   his wife
beats him with a kind
of swatter till his
blood runs. Hundreds of
children race about
the pasture   crying
"don't die   don't die."

she is frightened—
her ambition: is
it man-killing?

2

I'm cutting my naked lover's hair
in the bathroom. Suddenly
the scissors flash out to his prick.

she loves her love
she hates him—
she loves & hates
her need of him.

3

Inflated dolls: lifesize,
naked   with random tufts
of scraggly hair: someone
is showing me in an old
house empty of furniture.

daughters: will they go
naked because of
her alliance with
the devil, with power?

36

4

A wedding: two fat men
enter the church—
hold guns on us:
"Someone has raped
my virgin daughter—
drop your clothes—
we'll find out who."

I know who's guilty—
my dark father, son.
One slashes the legs
of a dark man, dissolves
his prick with acid.
I look over—my lover!
safe: light eyes, hair.

the man who loves her—
unless protected
by magic colors—
will he perish?

5

I have a son, a gorilla.
As large as I, he wrestles
me constantly. My lover says
I can give him away. *Release*
release: I haven't known it!

because of her love's aura
—half-man   half-woman—
her daughters are freed
she is loosed from night.

"Living on Rape Time"

If she's old enough to bleed, she's old
enough to butcher.
> *A fraternity member, Georgia*
> *Institute of Technology*

You drive into town—why? You don't take
the subway—why? You go to a certain
night school instead of another. Or you
don't go to night school at all. Or you go in
the daytime—why? All because of
rape—the fear of rape that dominates our
lives—and one day you get tired of living
on rape time!
> *A woman member of the Philadelphia*
> *rape squad, "Today" program,*
> *March 25, 1974*

the ultimate sex object: the victim of rape

1
Confidential   to the
Right Man   My One & Only

2
Are you a whip   a snake
a carver of hearts   over
my own: drawing the small
drops   an artist of
the red stars   that sting
burn   burst   from my eyes?

Are you chicano   black
bald   even (unbelievable)
blond: a Robert Redford
with the right credentials—
member of the hockey team
or even the rowing crew?

Are you the one who calls
from underground garages,
"Hey, senora   wanna fuck?"
Part of the gang in steel
& leather   straddling my
path on New York sidewalks?
The cabbie who murmurs as
we near my hotel, "Hey, baby,
won't you need me later?"
The cowboy in the bar—
cuddling your pistol   leering
as I order? The salesman
in the lobby   in wingtips
& pinstripes   laying a bill
in the bell clerk's palm?

Yes   who are you   who will
stand behind me   as I pull
out my key   as with fingers
gone slick   I labor the blade
you will twist from my palm
will press   sleight-of-hand
to the white of my neck?

3

As you wish   I've circled
my nipples in lipstick—
my mouth is ready for your prick—

I dream your blow in the belly—
the pillow held tight over
my face.   O my rapist

I am waiting for you
as for the perfect blind date
Prince Charming   the Right Man

my bridegroom made up as Dracula—
yes   beneath my jeans
my turtleneck   I wear

my pale bridal dress   a virgin's
trembling   and you know it:
how I believe in your coming

as I once did in Christ's—
in your gifts of blue bruises
red ribbons   starry looks—

in your jewelry of steel—
ice picks & razors   a Van Cleef
& Arpels array of them . . .

4

Even at breakfast   in a café
in Georgia   I'm surrounded
by you: tile layer   truck
driver   stacker of lead pipe—

I freeze into my lake
of grits   my snow white toast—
my newsprint articles on
cigarette burns   severed tits—

5

for whether walking out
of the New York Chelsea
Wyoming's Hawaiian Hilton
or the Fairyland Courts of
Lookout Mountain, Tennessee—
no matter how covered in
boots & sweaters   how many
times I answer, "I'm a school-

teacher"   alone   I'm guilty
of waiting for you in your
pickup   for the shotgun
you keep on the floorboard
for your tricks with corncobs
& coke bottles   for a get-
together with you & your gang—
yes   it's open season on me,
my pelt   and being woman,
Southern   I know my most
valuable part: the soft fur
at the base of my belly—
ripe for skinning   slashing
whatever you   my sweet   desires.

6

Vision: me sprawled over
the motel bedspread   my crotch
drooling   my legs spread—

Or folded into a tub—
hair flowing   eyes wide at
the sparkling porcelain of

Howard Johnson's: a good child
who has received her stars—
red   blue   gold   who now sleeps

the sleep of each of the eight—
those poor pure nurses   victims
of Amerika   of Richard Speck.

7

Weekly   I read articles
on "how to gouge"   devour
the pieces on "talking you

out of it"   practice my kicks
fifteen minutes a day—
and on the elevator   stare
toward your boots   flashing
your arm to my throat   our ride
to the basement   recalling
me   fourteen: in a road-
house near Stone Mountain   my
cheerleader's skirt shoved up
against wood so thick with
country sound as to drown
the tear of a whimper. In
girls brought up on Hank
Williams   revival meetings
the trade school boys in their
souped-up Chevies   knowledge
of our blood   never fully washed
away in His   is bred in.

    8

Still   I refuse to be ugly
for you: to let my lips chap
my belly go slack   to curl
my hair   or conceal my feet—
stranger   I'm learning to love
the stains I leave on motel
sheets   the syllables that
bubble on my lips   the drops
I will hurl to your face even
as you hurl me to concrete—
you the sophomore turned gang
banger   you the business
man looking for quick profit
you the cowboy as dumb as
the metal of your gun   yes

all you would-be John Waynes
of this world   I invite you:
ask the desk clerk to Xerox
my room number   the waiter
to give it out with the menus—
dear   the next time you leer
from an elevator   I'll enter
invite you   up   up   up
to my room to stroke the long
hidden edges   concealed
deep within my flesh—
to penetrate my cunt stuffed
with shards of real China
left from my mother's broken
life   the green splinters
my grandmother had to swallow
daily   the ground glass trapped
beneath the training bra
garter belt   the Barbie doll
curves of my long-gone teen-age
self: yes   love   my fingers
are ready for your ass—
my switchblade is oiled with
Vaseline: I am the doll
you will press   & instead
of real tears   the wetting
of panties   steel will spring
from my center   splitting
your prick   your balls   yes
my rapist   come up   come up
I'll take you on for all of
them: my grandmother   my mother
my daughter   my daughter's
daughter   all the women you've
done in & done in & done in.

The Amazon's Daughter

Leave your oppressive man for a beautiful
gay sister—come to the Sat nite dance at
141 Prince St D.O.B. *
*Women's rest room, Bleecker Street Theater,
New York City*

What holds women back from widespread
homosexuality? . . . To be loved by a
woman would mean to be loved by
someone as inferior as oneself.
Una Stannard, Women in Sexist Society

Women are Beautiful but I can't see
making it with a sister! SOME PEOPLE
JUST BELIEVE IN GIVING LIP
SERVICE
*Women's rest room, Mediterraneum Café,
Telegraph Avenue, Berkeley, California*

When shall we rejoice in the birth of
"divine" daughters? . . . How shall we
celebrate that day?
Phyllis Chesler

deep dreaming: the womb submerged

* Daughters of Bilitis

The Amazon's Daughter

In Amazon society there is no struggle . . .
except to resist invasion from the
foreigner. . . . A society without fathers,
brothers or sons. The intruder has been
totally removed. . . .
Jill Johnston, Lesbian Nation

Last night   daughter
I dreamed you a woman
who'd given birth:
naked   on your bed
with another girl
and from your vagina
into hers   a water-
fall poured   a silver-
sequined force   in
which a dozen tiny
men flailed arms and
legs   as helpless
as the GI Joes—
those plastic boys
in khaki suits—
you once forced in-
to intercourse with
Barbie   you once
hung by the neck
cut with razors
soothed with Mercur-
ochrome   their all-
powerful god-mother—

and today   through
a flash of door
I see into your

blood-red room—
its bureau-top
box of Tampax   as
in purple light
in Day Glo bath
you sit   naked
Indian-legged
on your single bed
painting nails
Mad Vermilion
Passion Purple—
dragging a toke
passing the joint
to your nude chum—
drowning in sandal-
wood   as Alice
murders his chickens.

Seeing your breasts—
cones of the bubble
gum ice cream you
still love   I recall
slumber parties way
back in the fifties
when we of the Secret
Seven   wore only
slips   smoked tobacco
cigarettes   unaware
of clitorises   talked
wedding styles   and
hymens   how far
to go   and when—
read from my parents'
dark book on sex—
memorizing positions
gasping at the weird

ones   till red-faced
near tears   we gouged
crotches with thumbs
big toes
            now daughter
as you   your friend
pass the roach in
a bobby pin   as
giggling   flashing
furry patches   you
begin to wrestle—
I watch your eyes
close & hers   hear
from out of doors
your cat tear apart
a bird: in squawks
and screeches   your
music rises   crests:
child   in this room
your temple   beneath
the swollen face of
Janis   every touch
is silken   every power
is female: small
men drown   forever.

Girl Friends

We canoe a creek
thick with half-dead
water moccasins,
as afraid of the boys
we're with as the snakes.

And grateful when both
our periods start at once:
in the outhouse
off the bathhouse
we stuff our panties

with stiff toilet paper,
dreaming we're back home
just the two of us—
playing strip poker
walking the railroad tracks

blouseless, smoking Kools
at the café in town.
Waiting for the pickups
we're terrified of
instead of these known

pimply-faced gluttons for
a bra-flip, a fingerfuck.

Oh, Men!

After Richard Wriggley
tore up my toy stove,
we went down to the sink-

hole. When he ripped the back
off a live turtle, I decided
men are beasts! And nine

confirmed it: Grady Looney
watched me kiss Tom on the lot
next door (empty, we thought)—

for months, he leered, I burned.
At recess, in fifth grade,
the boys would chase and hurt.

Each day, the girls had to fight
behind the monkey bars,
the swings: till back to class,

we held our noses as our common
loathing trooped up the aisles.
And twelve, Mother sent me

to the corner store, not knowing
every time I had to go,
the eighteen-year-old grocery

clerk whispered how he would
get me down and kiss me if we
ever met alone: one time, we

did, he did, I ran and ran.
At fifteen, in broader worlds,
I found that boys from the town

of Stone Mountain wore cowboy
boots on dates for church,
and after prayer, they hankered

not for the Blood of the Lamb,
but something similar. In school,
some boy whose back-seat touches

I had spurned would appear
in a hall to shout out loud,
"Pear-shaped, freckle-faced!"

My rounded flesh would crave
to cave, my freckles blaze
as cauterized, my pink

angora sweater flame. Even
the boys I had crushes on,
and kissed, might be enemies

underneath: strangers from
another race, like attractive
Martians. Now Hunky, Preacher,

blue jeans, abrasive beards,
Western boots and roaming hands
have transformed: friends are men,

and civilized. But sometimes,
as one suited, tied, holds my coat
and smiles, I retreat, afraid

his whispered words may be,
*"Pear-shaped, freckle-faced,
I'll get you yet!"*

Bridal Luncheon

We harness up our breasts,
sling beads upon our ears.
Now with slanted eyes we press
to find how she lured the prey.

She smiles a whiskered smile
that tells of vows she made:
his slaking of desire within
her curved and clawed embrace;

for this, he gives the stones,
the hut, the beads, forever.
Flashing diamond rings,
we toast the bride: so clever!

The ends of cigarettes glitter
redly from our fingertips.

Shiksa

They're pouring the gin, the tonic—
drinking, discussing the state of Boston—
your parents have clothes from Italy,
antiques, a town house on Marlborough Street.

Your *Georgia Peach*, I rest on the salt
of the Northeast, lick my lips over
derma, whitefish. Tropical, overripe,
rip lobsters from their shells, drip

butter and juices: a belle in a bell
jar, as pointing out the crown moldings,
your mother pulls her sweater down
over her hipbones, your brothers eye me,

your doctor-uncle thrusts his knee
between my thighs, talking neurology,
the dog, his namesake, tries rape: on a sea
of hostility, I'm floating, lightly.

Billet Doux to Miss Diamond

The desperate are dangerous; they must be
dealt with.

Glittery, hard-edged,
sharper than metal—
unset, unsettled, yet
never giving way:
the one desired girl
my bridegroom never
laid. Bitchy, a stone
gone slithery, a voice
on a telephone calling
to drip in a Milky Way
stream, all sparkly
(in a lighter mood,
for once, than suicide):
"Congratulations."
Come this way, sweetie,
and after forcing
your come on the bed
that's mine and his,
I'll crush your silver-
wrapped, cream-center
stone with its marshmallow
middle *inward*, proving
even a gem like you—
Clairgold hair, platinum
skin—is penetrable.

Talking of Stars

Talking softly of stars
we lie within our beds.

Nausea pulses my throat—
galaxies make me faint,
thinking how we float—
light things in shadowy
sheets.
      Later, wakening
from dreams of peacock wings

fluttered to dust ten thousand
years ago, I move through
quiet doors. In darkness,
my back presses the shivery
earth—
      with the old bone of
an animal, I love myself.

Rosemary

Rosemary.
Rosemary Hughes.
Rosemary Hughes Ramos
Rosemary Hughes Ramos Daniell
Rosemary Hughes Ramos Daniell Coppelman.
Rosemary Hughes Ramos Daniell
Rosemary Hughes Ramos
Rosemary Hughes
Rosemary who's?
Rosemary's.

Blood Sherbet

Woman's primary ego-identity is rooted in
a concern for limited and specific "others"
. . . [it] must somehow shift and be moored
upon what is necessary for her own
survival as a strong individual. . . . Such a
radical shift . . . grates and screeches
against the grain of all "feminine" nerves
and feelings, and implies grave retribution.
Some women go "mad" when they make
such a shift. . . .
Phyllis Chesler

freeze, and shattering

Blood Sherbet

The bush bends as beneath tragedy—
each branch, ice-capsuled.
Sticks glitter blue.
I stand without gloves—

the rose of my fingers turns to a blue
glass. My wrist could be slashed,
I would feel nothing.
My blood stands, unused plasma;

tears lie crystal beneath my cheekbones.
Like the bush, I am brittle,
captive of ice, prisoner of seasons.
Time twists, a Mobius strip—

daily, I await the slightest breach.

Mary, Mary

Mary was a sucker—
done in by the culture—
her role? to get screwed by God—
fall before His ghostly cock

then hang around the house
while the menfolks do their thing—
as carpenters, gurus—
her last scene?

a tableau: suffering over Him.
It goes on forever.

Tulips

The red head tilts—
alive, meaty.
I stoop to tear

a body thick
unwilling, yet
only dent it.

And watch tissue
lymph-filled,
the texture of

artichoke,
pour color
into air from

an opened oven.

Tiger Lilies

1

Are the plums on your tree ripe?
My fists hang like heavy pods.

2

And July, the blades of
curved leaves carve my legs.

In the pond, the swerve
of fish is turn, and twist.

The claws of tiger lilies
swipe my restless skirt.

3

In August, ripe things lapse.
Inside my chest, my heart

(out of step: still pumping)
is hacked by orange knives:

the hot maniacs of city
gardens: repeating, repeating.

A Bird Like a Peacock Downed

With a plop as soft,
as muffled as trauma,
I bring the bird down.

A beaked angel breaks
like bones through skin:
incredibly pure

and radiant. I
turn my prize with
a foot: feathers

change from jet
to purple to green,
to silver that draws

my sight. His visage
invites me enter
black slits struck through

yellow marble: the
temple of a Jehovah,
or devil. And something

like wind is murmuring,
"Pain is right.
I am made

for tearing apart."
And in incense of
blood released,

the sweet scent of
bestial flesh,
I gaze for hours

believing in the body
of my own passion.

The Rape of Lilith

Marry a castrating woman. But don't let
her.
    A psychotherapist to his male client

You are my puppet on the strings—
I hold the board above your head,
lick my lips, make you jerk.
Yet this power is not the one:
rather, to make you say and think,
to *be mine, mind,* my valentine,
my little man, my thing.

Inside my head is turned to "On,"
the switch, to "Power over Men"—
to break my father's back
with every lashing kiss:
my demon force, my black witch self,
my mother, smother love—
the kind that maims and kills—

computerized, long practiced.
O, I hate these filaments,
the mossy dirty underside of brain—
stalactites of skull, threads of adhesions—
twisted, ugly, purple.
Or a needle in the elbow, grown accustomed.
The witch is wound in her long hair,

yet the pain of motion is as always.
In the ocean of your gaze,
I fish for my will's gleam—
that sea turns dead, ceramic.
My brain coils, fury red—
Narcissus, Lilith never dreamed you,
who reach inside my head,

jerk out all the wires—
tangled, dripping blackened blood—
to toss them off our dais.
My toy, my lover boy, turns giant—
I fall, machine turned soft and slippery,
octopi without their fury—
now your will can ravish.

The Doll

For nothing can be sole or whole
That has not been rent.
  W. B. Yeats

Beneath yours, my painted eyes,
my sky-blue looks, turn to liquid.

On my perfect lips, my half-cries
turn spore and blood: I taste them.

Your fingers rake my molded slopes,
and lichen crawls across my chest.

Pores spring open, rubbers snap,
my sprung joints turn tender cartilage.

Your tongue plows my head, the underside
of my brain moves: I scream, "Ma-Ma!"

Your giant hands hold up my legs—
in your factory for unleashing,

things open up, synthetics melt.
Cells proliferate like killings.

You force caverns through Du Pont mountains.
And near my curls of nylon yellow,

volcanoes burst, lava spurts,
flesh turns sticky, raw things wiggle.

My lashes click through magic tears,
as lit by foxfire, phosphorescent,

the dream keeps on of plants underground
that open, shut, eating live things.

Where I was hollow, animals lurch.
Slick and arched, blue caves convulse.

Holiday Inn

Love has pitched his mansion
in the place of excrement.
    W. B. Yeats

Beginning with your fingers,
all cool things probe me—
blue lights, hard rubber, fixtures.
I see you coming in mirrors,
you rise behind me in warm water.

The walls are white oils,
I cannot reflect.
Am open here, forced into an operating theater,
exposed in a blue posture,
your eyes the eyes of a thousand students.

Something like light cartilage gives—
turning soft inside,
I hold the hard edge of a tub.
My forehead rests on tile.
Something goes on in the next room—

a salesman packs ashtrays and towels.
You take me and I cry:
in a room like this—
sleek, surface-perfect—
only I am porous.

The Victim

When the children are born, the parents
begin to die.
    Hegel

1
Beautiful cannibals are eating me.

What nourishes their flesh is mine—
the organ meats, the juiciest tidbits—
liver, or eyeballs. They eat their house,

break in the sides, rip out the roof beams.
I am the walls that are crashing—
I am falling, I am falling, I am gone.

2
Innocent infants, they hung about my neck

like wet sacks, or small chimps. Opened their mouths
like birds: I thrust in the delicate spoonfuls—
hearts beat fast beneath their snowsuits.

Till, at the end of their meal, having probed
my entrails for more, they discuss tying strings
to my thumbnails, riding away on bicycles.

3
Naïvely, I assumed they were friendly—

yet these strangers let in on a Sunday morning
for coffee and cake hold the knife to my throat—
I should have known when they carried only

the heads of dolls in the grocery carts.
Roasting caterpillars over open fires,
pulling the claws from crayfish was child's play.

4

Now with the skeleton of me left—

the shredded muscle, the hanging eyeball—
should I rely at last on instinct?
Throw the TV set through a window,

wring the necks of the pets, crush the soft
spots turned iron? Rage, like a magician's
power, flows from my fingertips:

5

I will fly apart, or they will.

Georgia History

(& the Coast off Newfoundland)

In the mid-nineteenth century in
Washington, Georgia, a town known for its
columned (and decaying) mansions and
magnolia-lined avenues, a woman was
hanged wearing her best white silk dress.
At the urgings of wives jealous of her
beauty, jurors had found her guilty of the
murder of her husband.

Off Newfoundland, in April, [hunters] are
allowed one day to kill infant seals and
their mothers.
        Life *Magazine, March 21, 1969*

1

Woman hangs from
a tree in bloom.

2

Off Newfoundland
in April   snowy
babies blossom red

3

as on this coast—
this Miami Beach—
in this harem—
blinding sand—
perfect light—
Mother sunbathes:
camellia cream—
a natural blonde—
still believing
white fur on white

snow   can save—
THE STUPID CUNT!
A cow can't know
the magic of gun-
sights   till juice-
jeweled   she's hooked—
Dolly on a dolly—
a rich desirable
matron   CAMERAS
ROLL: as hangdog
her flippers dangle—
fat is stylish here—
it makes a killing!

4

O her blond girl
is locked out—
the tomahawks
descend too fast!

Her sweet pearl brooch
turns rag doll left
out in blood-rain:
sodden   muscle-blooming

5

as the dogwood coast
off Newfoundland
sings   the place
explodes: beyond
the dazzle of
white   a festival—
a crystal float
a garden of poppies
anemones   a symphony
of whimpers   O

a spring jamboree!
Lush reds spurt
slush flowers skulls
sun gods with long
oaken arms stand
in ice water—
in blood steam—
clubbing daughters
clubbing daughters.

The State of Georgia

(August 1969)

By the power invested in me by the state
of Georgia, I pronounce you woman and
life. . . .

1

O this place is my state
of perpetual Mickey Mouse—
a shape on a map, the south
of an old whore, a hole plugged
with excrement, a moist rotten
splotch under the skirts of
America: not decently
east, nor cleanly west—

in Georgia, in August, woman
cannot afford disbelief
in Salvation by the Blood
that flows slow as sorghum—
in Jesus, the savior of whites,
of Mary Magdalene & all defiled. . . .

2

At two A.M., slugs streak
across the floor near the sink.
Out of my white-hot shrouds, off
a mattress shoved to the floor

I step on one, dreaming how
this moment, maggots move beneath
the back wooden steps, the mercury
reads one hundred two, crawls
toward the line of high blood . . .

and push the screen of the door
to walk over tiger lilies
gone slick & brown. Kudzu—
an arm, a boa constrictor—
squeezes out thought. As dumb
as a mongoloid, I pause

near the tropic of garbage—
the tampons, melting boxes—
the rind of my breakfast peach
feeds a dozen pale bodies:

more slugs lay chains of glitter,
and I, too, weave moonside out,
an animal secreting silver—

unclean, as are all creatures
here, I simmer, rot & await

3
the gun of a deadly September,
the act by which I shall be freed.

Declaration Day

(July 4 in Georgia, 1969)

1
Kudzu: a weed brought
to Georgia from Japan:
vines thick as tree trunks,
covering mountains—

turning woods jungle—
here, men walk fifty
feet up, the bodies
of women are buried.

2
Glossalia, or speaking in tongues.
Time swells like watermelon,
heat greases the garden wall,
grasses in the garden grow
tall, tall. In the south
can be no Independence Day—
lethargy strangles like kudzu,
covers my sex as I sleep, as
I lie beside you unwilling,
dreaming how I will speak—
o to open my mouth will take
an air not in this place—
for here at dawn the hum
of crickets is a blanket—
yes, to move will take
the courage of a revolution—
to hurt, to cut through snakes.

3

Divorce: tearing off
an adhesive bandage
full of hair & raw flesh.

Love: an artery turned
aneurysm, burst dam—
persistently, I see red.

4

Morning.   Bouncing a red
ball, our daughter comes into
our room in an orange smock.
A clot throbs in the part
of my head that dreams. Red
smears my thigh: last night,
I returned to this house,
and in the tangle of sheets,
my womb shed its lining. O
my heart is a strawberry
bleeding (that fragile), a shape
loosing soft beds and old
beginnings. Now the child
leaves the room, and I beg
for divorce the way one dying
of cancer begs for morphine.

5

Bleeding: a sign of fertility or cancer?
(Blood in the diaphragm, fear in the bathroom.)

6

release me   release me   I
am blind with widening vessels
bruises from ten years back ache
embolism shudders and threatens

hemorrhages of feeling   a hemophilia
that will not stop till you do
a blood-letting   an episiotomy:
I am primipara   giving birth
to freedom as one births a child:
in labor   through pain   still
your erection is unbelieving

7
Taught as a child:
to kill snakes, a sin.
In kudzu, the snouts
of hogs root them.

8
As I rest on the couch
you come, place a hand
on my breast, will not stop
though I beg. And turn me into
an old woman, drooly, teary—
bleeding with cancer & piles.
Or a child with a daddy
who insists on his incest.
My gashes ache, both of them.
Yet over a revolt of the heart
my breasts clench, my fists
tighten. I insist. I scream.

A Sexual
Tour of the
Deep South

Do yo' know where yo' wound is?
Housemaid, describing method of home abortion

. . . it looked like it was a foot long, and
felt like it was ten!
*Fifteen-year-old bride of a week, describing her
wedding night to girl friends in the yard of an
Atlanta Church of God prior to Sunday morning
services*

I sometimes wonder if the late J.C. was a
good lay? SOME PEOPLE SURE
WISH THEY COULD GET MORE
IN TOUCH WITH GOD!
*Corresponding graffiti, women's rest room,
neighborhood bar, Atlanta*

Smile—God loves you even if the boys
don't!
*Girls' rest room, junior high school, Duluth,
Georgia*

Over Chattanooga*

"She'll turn from beauty to beast before your eyes!"
In kelly suit, zircon rings, dark and fat, he yells,
"She'll moan, she'll groan, she'll kick the dust!"
A kewpie cracks in my sweated grasp: I know he
is shouting of me, the people of the fair turn to look:
the farmers, the housewives, the 4-H'ers, the businessmen
who run stores and own banks. For as I walk this
corridor of sawdust, clutching my soft bear, my doll,
concession hawkers call out to me, stretch their long arms
and whistle, "Here, little girl, come over here—
I've got something to give you: nine inches of gristle!"
They call through my clothes, they call into my open parts,
dreaming my awful desires. I stare into the glass eye
of my bear, still seeing from the corner of vision,
a huge tattoo quiver, move on a beckoning muscle.
The eagle flies under my dress, flutters between
my thighs: to be fifteen is to fear rising, to lie
in my bed and fear descending, the reward of raising
my mouth in the back seat of an old Chevrolet, smelling
of grease and brake fluid, punishment for the upward
floating of my pink angora sweater, over a breast,
of drifting out the car window as my real flesh
lay impaled. Knowing that as I let myself in at one,
I will peel my clothing in darkness, the kitten-soft sweater
turned evil, a witch's garment deserving of flame—
to slip between quilts beside my hairless younger sister,
still dreamless from watching Milton Berle on TV,
to squirm, to sizzle till morning.
                                        Yes, this moment,
in the house of mirrors, I see the frothy rotting brain
beneath my freckles, the layer of green mold beneath

---

* At a fair in Chattanooga, Tennessee, a teen-age girl died when the chained
swing in which she was riding broke loose and flew out over the fairgrounds.

my peroxided hair. This boy Hollis slides his arm
around me: I turn fat   thin   a hunchback   a dwarf.
His hand drops to my gathered skirt: my face changes,
recalling the treadle on grandmother's machine   going in
and out   down and up. His fingers mash:

                              on the merry-
go-round, I ride water moccasins   red hound bitches
sows in heat. As Hollis walks me toward the exhibit
of beasts, I search the blue eyes of my doll, knowing
how the hogs   the bulls   the horses   with their terrible
glowing pricks, will breathe me, and will leap like light,
a half a ton heavier than the sawdusty dog that drags
at my socks. Candied apples, sweet things, smear my teeth.
Behind halos of sugary pink, the faces of the good
rise, the music of the jukebox tells them how I'll "never
make a wife for a home-lov-in' man. . . ." O even the
lobster-man, flapping across the sideshow stage in her gown
of purple satin, is less garish than I am: quick   Jesus
Hollis   I want to find the scariest ride and ride it
alone.
      The chained swing. Once at Jacksonville Beach,
I almost drowned. Salt went down my throat like the taste
of a boy when my hair is caught in his fist. Then I gagged
and Jesus, I do now, recalling that one vacation trip
when my baby sister and I rode the waves   down and up
hearing from the boardwalk the sound of how I could have
"turn-ed to a honk-y tonk wo-man. . . ."   And later, on that
sloping sidewalk, I became a doll that moved by momentum,
a shape that couldn't help it, swerving toward the hands
of the men as I have tonight at this fair, where with
a machine that spins without mercy, in this seat of dark
brown plastic, sticky with bits of Moon Pie, spilled Big Orange,
my evil half-smeared monthly blood, I fly beyond what
I've known: away   away   close   close. Choking on air,
I vomit it: onto my home ec blouse, into my green tangling

hair. At my ankle, a bracelet of tin, two hearts entwined,
burns to bone, the world turns flat
                              Jesus, I'm afraid
it's as if I'm singing in the choir of Your house
the flesh of my face filling up with the Blood I should
have been washed in, as dipped in Your burning waters
in the creek at the back of Your house, I thought not of purity
but the peach flesh beneath my wet white dress, of rising
with the nipples of a siren: shivering, clearly possessed;
how even during prayer, my eyes would fall like a witch's
onto the thigh of some boy, my thoughts to what might come
later—no, Lord, not thinking of You at all, but rather
how in need of loosening lay my bones, how fast
the football player   the boy from the filling station
the sailor just back from Korea   could cover himself
in rubber
              yes, Jesus, I'm sorry   sorry   yet glad
that my kewpie crumbles to bloodless bits of plaster
that my bear flies to dust in the air   that saving
my Mama, my sweet baby sister from grief   this swing
on chains lifts me toward a guiltless love, a marriage.
That over a quickening quiet, I ride in this chair
like a throne   that the bar I've finally lifted sets me
free from this sail plane coffin   this body of flesh
that my tearing skirt   my rotten legs   slide helpless
from metal   till I break at the waist   my ugly parts
fly away like the chaff   *Jesus, pierce my forehead*
with thorns   bushes   whole trees: I'm coming at last

In Grady Hospital

I was sinking deep in sin, far from the
peaceful shore, when He came and took me
in . . . then love lifted me. . . .
    Baptist hymn

Taken at my supper of sorghum and biscuit,
driven in the back of Pa's old pickup—
shed of my feedsack dress, my belly shaved,
my bowels forced—I lie in this public place:

it's the night before my sixteenth birthday
and all memory is in a bed like a cage,
on this table like a made-up tombstone,
in the black who mops the tiles as I beg. . . .

Already, women in white, old aunts or virgins,
have arranged their hoses, tightened my straps,
pushed up my clothes, exposed me to the blond one
who teased, "Girl, this is no baby, but a lump. . . ."

Who with a finger gone slick probed deep
my animal shame, who needled my arm
for blood just as what's in me clawed *out*.
All night, Lord, I've searched Your red words,

turned the gold edges of Your promises—
still, the pictures I see are me, my panties
from Kresge's a mound on the straw. Or now:
grabbing up one of their blades, tearing this

poor thing from my belly. Dreams are knives:
o the end of it, the end of it: that Pa
had done what he started: got down his shotgun,
stuck it up me, pulled the trigger. For as

Your fist squeezes this balloon to marble,
as Pepsi creeps between my picked chicken parts,
something shoves toward its door to the world:
beneath needles like nails   in mirrors boiling red

I become the crucified   Your blood gone clear
pours from my palms   my wrists twist in leather
that ties me to fire   to something that has been
is   will be: O LORD GOD JESUS PA

IN YOUR ARMS   ON A WHITE CLOUD   LIFT ME

The Bible Salesman

A sound on wood breaks late morning sleep.
Loosed from the weight of the walrus-man,
the house lights on its stilts of brick.
And dreaming of knives, still in the spin
of the board she is strapped upon,
her wrists wired by the line for clothes,
the blades just missing the place in her groin—

Delilah, of comic books, in a black suit, skin-tight.
But this sound commands she rise from the
    thread-edged spread,
to move in her dress of night, not jet, but blue—
voluminous, to cover her wrong-filled form.
To look blindly out her corrugated face,
printed by stitches of designs on chenille—
to rush in her thin, translucent skin
with weight, a thrown knife's directness.

Yet with touch the knob moves from her,
swings as a door onto heaven:
with what must be the largeness of God,
a man by his height ascends, fills up the porous frame—
cheeks sun-blazed, a Bible rides his golden arm,
a bulge shining as through righteousness.
Before the halo that eats the East,
the curls of his head change into circles.

Surely an angel leans toward her,
come to release her from midways, from danger.
Yes, he opens Old Testaments and sings,
"Lady, let me sell you salvation.
Let my power stop what gores without mercy.
Freedom from knives, sticking the flesh of your thigh—
O here, hear the Song of Solomon."

Divinely guided, he moves.
The couch bends with the weight of his radiance,
the can beneath a corner is light-struck,
the hairs of his arm pull flame through the window.
Forced in the field of magnets, she slides,
his fingers flicking the pages of leaf
as surely as wings move for their motion.
His gaze draws up hers as through metal.

Gold-edged, words dissolve from her vision—
without breath, something is melting
like cotton candy in the warmth of her mouth.
She knows herself falling, kneeling,
she hears her own speech begging—
her face presses the dark of his lap.
"O Lord, this must be the one:
Over the hearts of men,
His very books stop bullets."

Lo, he stiffens with love and wrath,
his soft light becomes as a staff—
from her straps, her board, she floats,
with sudden ascension, shuddering.
She flies from the shrouds of her night dress,
the dark blue mounds at his feet.
Freed from corsets, from wires, she soars,
impaled and let loose at once,

as though he has raised her high,
his voice declaiming in liquid,
"Only the sensual are innocent."
The tongue of the angel whirls in her earlobe:
And hollow, lightened, she changes to vessel.
"David learned to love God," he whispers.
The carousel music crashes.

And clothed in his one light hair, she lies in a new sleep,
    dreamless.
Beneath the layers of dozing, the tender sound of a door
    closing,
she knows she will hold this knowledge like Christ's mother,
for when, in covers of darkness, the walrus-man moves,
limbless, heavily flapping—or while, with new light belly,
she serves the cornbread, the cabbage:
that the carnival dream never comes twice.
That her sin has been accomplished.

Cullasaja* Gorge

Heavy with what was conceived
the day she was born in Georgia Baptist Hospital,
she drags her sin to North Carolina.
It pulls like tar to her every heel-step,
weighs down the car she drives up mountain.
Inside her white woman shape, a wolf-man growls.

The bulk of her monster pulls toward cliffsides:
Callasaja Gorge moves on her will,
the green-black ravine draws like God's magnet.
Voices rise from the feathered caverns,
"Woman, flowers grow to cover your rottenness.
Stones are sharp to open your belly,

to let sun burn on slime and dankness."
A wave of salt breaks her makeup,
her hand forces the slickening wheel:
the next moment, she could be free of it.
She teeters on edges, held in place by a rock,
dreaming her car, mashed like a toy—the scales

of her garments peeled, the beast within her, dead.
Yes, she can rise as a ghost. Or return
to the streets of Atlanta, virgin—
as pure as a debutante, in grace again—
first, she must find the act that can free her,
more unnatural than what slobbers within.

Beneath glass, like a weighted doll, she makes her car crawl
upward, toward Bridal Veil Falls.
Her hair man, her hermaphrodite itches:
beyond the net of falling water, a parked Chevrolet sparkles,

* Cherokee word for "sweet."

and struck all over the paint of silver
are labels, signs, singing: "The Blood

of Jesus Is the Only Way   FEEL DON'T THINK
see the bear see the snake   real Amazing Grace."
Her eyes lash toward the man who sits on the hood
like a savior: sweat-radiant, hawk-nosed
on high—who leans toward the great cross of gilt
strapped by leather to the shimmering ark,

till his shirt-sleeved arms glisten like icons,
the hairs spring like grounded coils.
And pushed by the body of her sin,
she swings the door of her Triumph—
through her shirt, his eyes fasten to it—
her thin soles slide on uneven granite.

She falls to her knees, he laughs, his leaded
thumb presses the back of her neck.
His eyes into hers, she wrenches it out:
the body of her sin jerks up her throat,
tears through her mouth in the shape of a scream.
The flesh of the wolf-man is bitter on her tongue.

Near, now afar, she hears the crash of the beast
through brush. And skinless, skirtless, lies in a heap—
uncaring that fingers as yellow as those of a heathen,
that a ring of zircon, as sharp as a diamond,
scissor her new purity. That an unholy sweat,
wine turned sour, smears her mouth.

As speaking in tongues, her wounded lips caw
of deliverance: a liturgy let down from the glistening labels:
"FEEL OF IT SMELL OF IT TASTE OF IT   jesus jesus jesus
Just as I Am, without one plea   BUT THAT THY BLOOD
  WAS SHED."

Her eyelids flicker toward rayon knees—
the motor of the silver thing grinds like a plane—

the voice of God's man descends from above: "You can
get up now, sister." And shriven of lust by lust—
with new lightness, like a woman hours after birth,
she rises to wash in the tender water.
The Bridal Veil Falls heals what was torn.
Shaking her sparkling, mica-filled skirt,

she dreams the icon dragged up mountain:
the moving temple, blazing its message.
Behind the effortless wheel of her Triumph,
she floats down mountain toward Atlanta, sinless.

The Angel Stud

To seal sunlight out of this room,
I pull down the shade with a hand:
women have a special relation to water,
and today, a heavy river glides through my tissues,
makes me lie down on the spread of chenille:

to float out midday beneath an old blanket of Orlon—
to feel, beyond the tingling of fiber,
a melting of ice, a crumbling.
Like figs in my basement jar,
caught in their syrup of gloss,

I have waited all winter through darkness—
in the middle of naps that Southern women take,
he returns to those who believe him:
he descends like an aura to the field of flesh.
And this day, through thin skin lids,

I watch the light fixture of coned metal lower,
turn to the curves of the god-man,
the shade shapes to his face.
O, a great horse breaks through the hedge of my sleep,
he splashes at the edge of softening ice.

My stream surges, comes out my lips in gurgles.
He touches my hand and draws it,
the end of his tongue licks my palm,
slips to the joining of fingers—
he pours himself into my keeping,

and my mouth becomes a soft marsh like the wet earth near rivers.
At the brush of his weightless haunches,
I well with the delight of reunions—

words become mouthings of damp sounds.
We travel together on waves of light and water

that rise and fall to headlong lasers:
the horse gallops through the deep part so fast,
his hooves break up the small pebbles!
And freed of the light bones of myself,
like a yeast let loose by succulent warmth,

my spirit rises: even from his clasp, I dissolve—
and hearing my own cries,
lift through a tangle of Orlon,
eyelids finally refloating,
to see in the dresser mirror, a radiance,

like flecks of light foam, lit on a lip, stuck to a breast.
And know today, bread dough will slide from my fingers,
the stove will be soft and malleable.
And tonight, touched by the Angel Stud,
I will know how to flow toward a man.

About the Author

Rosemary Daniell's poems have appeared in the *Atlantic Monthly, New York Quarterly*, other magazines, and anthologies. In 1974, she received a National Endowment for the Arts grant in literature. A native of Atlanta, Ms. Daniell has worked as a mother of three, journalist, advertising copywriter, poetry reviewer, teacher of poetry workshops, and program director for Georgia's Poetry in the Schools program.